How
Finance Themselves

FINANCING OPTIONS AT VARIOUS STAGES OF DEVELOPMENT AND PRODUCTION

Mariusz Skonieczny

Investment Publishing

MISHAWAKA, INDIANA

Mariusz Skonieczny/Investment Publishing

1202 Far Pond Cir

Mishawaka, IN 46544

www.classicvalueinvestors.com

Ordering Information:

Quantity sales. Special discounts are available on quantity purchases by corporations, associations, and others. For details, contact the "Special Sales Department" at the address above.

How Gold Companies Finance Themselves/Mariusz Skonieczny. —1st ed.

ISBN 978-0-9848490-5-5

Table of Contents

Preface

Preface

WHEN I FIRST STARTED investing in gold mining stocks, I was surprised how little information was available for investors to learn about these businesses. Yes, there were some technical books, but they were mostly written in a way that would put anybody to sleep very quickly. Don't ever ask an engineer to teach you about the gold mining business, unless, of course, you are an engineer yourself. That's the only way you will understand what he or she is saying. And don't ask the CEOs about their businesses—they will just confuse you more than help you.

Because there was so little available, I felt there was a need for some books about the gold mining industry in layman's terms. In my first book on the topic, *Gold Production from Beginning to End*, I discussed what gold companies do to produce an ounce of gold. In this book, I focus on the financing side of the gold business. It is a topic that is especially important for gold mining companies because they are extremely capital intensive. I highly encourage you to read *Gold Production from Beginning to End* first because it will help you understand many terms that I use in this book.

Like information on gold production, the information available on financing is limited. I don't want to mislead you—the knowledge and information is out there, but it is not available in a top-down, easy-to-understand format. One source might have information about equity financing and convertible debt, and another source might explain streaming and joint ventures. However, they leave you wondering how it all fits into the big picture. The information is scattered around.

If you own stock in a particular gold company, you should be able to find out what kind of financing options the company has and why. If you can't, then how will you know that the company will survive? You need to have this basic knowledge because capital funding is the lifeblood of this business. Nothing gets done without huge amounts of capital.

The purpose of this book is to give you the big picture. You will learn about the types of financing options available and which types of companies have access to them. For example, one company might have the option of using debt, equity, or alternative financing, while another company might only be able to use equity. Or it might not be able to get financing at all, and as a result, its stock will go to zero.

I am not a finance guy. I am simply an investor that was frustrated with the lack of good information. Also, other investors kept asking me how they could learn about not only the gold mining business in general, but also the finance side of it. I wished there were some books that I could recommend to them, but unfortunately I was not satisfied with anything on the market. My intent is for *Gold Production from Beginning to End* and *How Gold Companies Finance Themselves* to fill that gap.

Introduction

Introduction

IT IS NO SECRET that the gold mining industry is capital intensive. It costs millions, hundreds of millions, and even billions to put mining projects into production. Every single step of the way, whether it is exploration drilling or mine construction, requires lots of capital. Consequently, mining companies have to be good at raising capital to progress themselves and their projects. There are four types of capital sources:

- Internal funds
- Equity
- Debt
- Alternative financing

Internal Funds

Internal funds come from cash flows generated by operating mines or property sales. These funds can be used to further expand production or resources. They can also be used to acquire other projects.

Internal funds in the form of cash flows are the most desirable form of financing because they do not require approval from third parties. How the money is spent is completely at the discretion of the management. Shareholders do not have to get diluted and companies do not have to leverage themselves. While internally generated cash flows from producing mines are the best, only producers can have them—exploration and development companies are excluded.

For the non-producers, internally generated funds can come from selling properties. It is not unusual for gold companies to own several projects. Selling some of them to other companies is a way to raise money for the development of the remaining projects. While this type of financing does not dilute existing shareholders, it does shrink the assets base.

For example, Goldgroup Mining, a company with operations in Mexico, had three projects: Cerro Prieto, Caballo Blanco, and San José de Gracia. None of the projects were generating meaningful cash flows so the company needed to sacrifice one in order to have enough capital to develop one or both of the other projects. Consequently, the management decided to sell Caballo Blanco for $30 million and use the funds to develop Cerro Prieto and San José de Gracia further towards production. The company could have looked for other financing methods, but it chose this one because equity financing was too dilutive (the stock price was too cheap) and debt financing was not available.

Equity

Companies that do not generate any cash flow and do not have or want to sell other properties have to rely on other sources of capital. This includes equity financing, which is the most common type of financing. It is available to all gold mining or exploration companies regardless of whether they are exploring, developing, or producing. So, as you can see, producing companies have more financing options while non-producing companies might have equity as their only financing option. Usually, there is no way for a junior exploration company to raise debt financing when it has no revenues.

Equity financing is raising capital from existing shareholders/owners or new shareholders. It is done through the issuance of new or additional shares. Obviously, equity raising is the most dilutive of all financing options, but, at the same time, it grows the assets base with the capital raised. It also does not increase risk by leveraging the company.

Debt

Debt, on the other hand, is the least dilutive financing option, but it is only available to companies that are already producing, are about to produce, or can demonstrate that they have solid collateral. Debt lenders are the most risk averse, and they want to make sure that they will get their money back with interest.

Companies that have mines that are already producing are able to demonstrate to lenders that they have the ability to repay a loan and make monthly payments. A company like this can also use its producing mine as collateral to obtain a loan. It can then use the money from the loan to expand production on the producing mine, or to develop a different mine that is not yet in production.

Gold mining companies that are about to produce can also use debt to finance the development and construction of their properties so that they can be turned into revenue-generating mines. For this to happen, they have to complete feasibility studies that describe in detail and prove through testing how the projects are going to generate cash flows high enough to repay the loan.

In certain cases, other less advanced companies can also use debt financing, but they have to demonstrate that the value of their properties is high enough to satisfy the lender's collateral requirement.

For example, Goldgroup Mining was able to get a $10 million loan to advance Cerro Prieto toward production. The company was able to get debt financing because the value of its other property, Caballo Blanco, was high enough that the lender was not worried about a default.

Alternative Financing

Equity and debt financing have their advantages and disadvantages. Equity can be dilutive and expensive, and sometimes, even unavailable during terrible bear markets like the one we are experiencing as I am writing this book. Debt, while non-dilutive, is risky because bankers want their money back even if there are delays in production, cost overruns, and sharp declines in the price of gold.

Consequently, gold companies may turn to alternative financing sources, such as royalty, streaming, or strategic agreements. Royalty deals involve getting an up-front lump sum payment from a royalty company in return for giving up a small percentage of revenue or profits generated from future gold production. Streaming deals involve getting an up-front payment or a series of payments based on various milestones reached in return for selling, at a fixed price, a portion of future gold production or by-product production like copper or silver. Strategic agreements involve partnering with capital-rich companies and selling them part of a project.

The benefit of alternative financing agreements is that they do not dilute existing shareholders or increase risk, but they do dilute the future cash flow that will be derived from the projects.

Summary

Gold companies are capital-intensive beasts. Without capital, they cannot progress their projects. There are four sources of funding available to gold mining companies. Some companies, such as explorers, can access only one type of financing while others, such as producers, can have it all.

Consequently, I divided the book into four main parts:

- Explorers
- Evaluators
- Developers
- Producers

Within each section, I discuss the kind of financing options that are available to each group. As I move up the ladder, I will not repeat myself. For example, if I already talked about equity financing in the Explorers chapter, I will not discuss it in detail in the Developers chapter. Whatever financing options I discuss in one chapter also apply in later chapters.

Financing Options

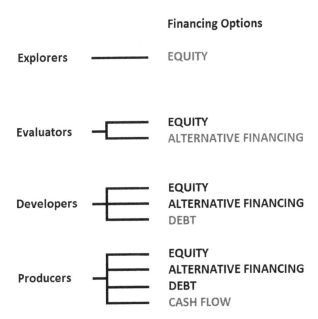

Explorers — EQUITY

Evaluators
EQUITY
ALTERNATIVE FINANCING

Developers
EQUITY
ALTERNATIVE FINANCING
DEBT

Producers
EQUITY
ALTERNATIVE FINANCING
DEBT
CASH FLOW

CHAPTER 1

Exploration

CHAPTER 1

Exploration

GOLD EXPLORATION is the first step in the gold production process. It involves looking for gold by first identifying where to drill, and then, drilling deep inside the earth to get rock samples.

Diamond Drill Core Samples

These rock samples are used to determine whether gold is present. All of the activities required to search for the yellow metal cost a lot of money. For example, one meter of diamond drilling can cost between $75 and $200, so a 20,000-meter drill program can cost $2 million. Someone has to pay for it, and it is not going to be a bank.

Think about it for a second. Companies that are searching for gold have nothing. They have no assets. It is funny because some investors buy gold exploration companies because they believe that the price of gold will go up. Well, exploration companies do not have any gold. They are searching for it.

Because they have no valuable assets, banks cannot lend to them. There is no collateral. This is why investing in exploration-only companies is speculative—it is difficult to assess the underlying value.

As a result, companies in the exploratory stage can only finance their operations through the issuance of equity. But before they seek financing, how do they come into existence? An individual, usually a geologist, or a group of individuals acquire an exploration property and incorporate as a private company. Then, they have to raise some serious money because nothing meaningful can be accomplished without it.

At that point, they face a decision—go public or stay private.

Many would prefer to stay private because it is cheaper and has fewer hassles, but outside investors are unlikely to invest in their ventures if they have no way to sell shares. Yes, these investors *could* sell their shares, but only if they found a buyer themselves, which is just too much bother for most people.

Consequently, many gold exploration companies go public at an early stage in order to raise the necessary funds.

When going public, they also have several choices. They can list the company on an exchange without raising funds, which, for most, is pointless considering the whole point is to raise money. So, they list on an exchange with concurrent public fundraising, meaning a traditional initial public offering, or IPO. This is by far the most popular route. However, they can also get creative by orchestrating a reverse takeover or a qualifying transaction with a capital pool company (CPC).

A reverse takeover happens when a private company gets acquired by a public company trading on a particular exchange and the shareholders of the private company become majority shareholders of the newly formed entity.

Canada's TSX Venture Exchange (TSXV), has a program that it calls the "capital pool company program" specifically for this type of reverse takeover. Some other exchanges have similar programs. The capital pool company is simply a shell with cash. It went public with the sole purpose of finding and acquiring another company.

The TSXV's capital pool company program involves two stages: first, the capital pool company files a prospectus, completes its IPO, and acquires its listing; second, it acquires another company or asset in what is called a "qualifying transaction." The TSXV has rules regarding how many shares can be sold, how much capital can be raised, and how much time the shell company has to find another company or asset to acquire.

Two of the biggest benefits for a company being acquired are that it can obtain financing earlier and at less cost than it could if it were to go public through an IPO itself. The owners of the capital pool company receive a percentage ownership in the new entity depending on how much value they brought to the table.

Traditional IPO

A traditional IPO usually involves the preparation of a prospectus in accordance with rules designated by particular exchanges and the regulators that oversee them.

Because exploration companies do not generate any revenues, they are not really businesses. They are just shell companies with "hope" assets and cash ready to burn. Therefore, they cannot be picky about which exchanges they float their shares on. Traditional exchanges like the NYSE or NASDAQ want nothing to do with them.

Luckily, there are exchanges that cater to them, such as the TSXV, AIM (Alternative Investment Market), and ASX (Australian Securities Exchange).

TSX and TSX Venture

Canada is the leading country when it comes to raising money for mineral exploration and development companies. It is home to the Toronto Stock Exchange (TSX) and TSX Venture Exchange (TSXV), which are operated by the TMX Group, Inc.

The TSX, TSXV, ASX, and AIM are the top exchanges for mining companies. Of the total number of mining companies listed on these exchanges, approximately 60 percent are listed on the TSX and TSXV, roughly 34 percent are listed on the ASX, and just under 6 percent are listed on AIM. A few are listed on the NYSE/NYSE MKT, HKEX (Hong Kong Exchange), JSE (Johannesburg Stock Exchange), and the LSE. In 2015, 53 percent of the global mining financings were done on the TSX and TSXV, according to the TMX Group.

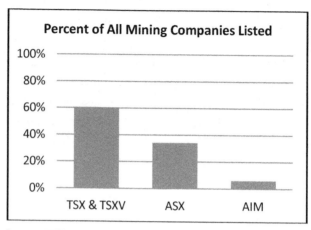

Percent of All Mining Companies Listed

Sources: TSX Inc., ASX Limited, London Stock Exchange plc.

Because of Canada's proximity to the United States, TSX- and TSXV-listed companies also have access to all of the North American capital markets.

The TSX is considered the main or senior exchange and only more established companies are able to meet the exchange's listing requirements. Early-stage companies go with the TSXV, which caters to smaller enterprises and is a sister exchange to the TSX. However, it is not just for mining. The TSXV has been a destination for all kinds of companies in developmental stages, such as ones in the oil and gas, industrial, and service industries. However, mining is the most popular.

On the Venture exchange, companies can typically raise between $500,000 and $20 million, which is not enough to build a mine but which is enough for a full or partial drilling program. Many have the goal of being able to eventually move their listings to the TSX, where they can raise significantly more money for the construction, expansion, or acquisition of a mine.

The TSXV has minimal listing requirements in order to facilitate startups. For those new to the exploration business, these requirements are surprisingly low. For example, there is no requirement for any net tangible assets or the ability to generate revenues or earnings. The requirement for working capital is that it needs to be enough to last for 12 months.

To start the listing process on the TSXV, a company has to submit a listing application describing how it meets the listing requirements and file a prospectus. The prospectus is a document that contains a description of the history of the company and its operations, financial statements, and a business plan. It also includes the intended use of the proceeds from the share issuance, and biographical descriptions of officers, directors, and major shareholders.

While the Canadian securities authorities are reviewing the preliminary prospectus, the company uses it to market itself to prospective investors. When the preliminary prospectus is approved, the final prospectus is filed and the listing candidate can finally gain access to precious capital by selling shares to the public.

However, with this access comes the responsibility of complying with quarterly financial reporting requirements, providing material corporate updates and investor relations communications, and reporting insider transactions.

From the day that an entity becomes public, there is no privacy. Everything is on display. This is one of the reasons why many founders would prefer to keep their enterprises private. But like I said before, being public allows a company to have much easier access to capital.

While the reporting requirements to maintain a public listing on the TSXV increase general and administrative expenses, they are nothing compared to what companies listed on US exchanges have to go through because of the Sarbanes-Oxley Act.

AIM

The London Stock Exchange (LSE) is another attractive destination for gold mining companies to go public and satisfy their capital needs. The LSE and AIM, which is a submarket of the LSE, are kind of like the TSX and TSXV in that between the two, the LSE is the choice for the established mining companies, while AIM serves the small and less established names. AIM tends to attract European and African issuers.

While AIM is an alternative listing destination, it is not as popular as its Canadian competitors. The TSX and TSXV have a tremendous advantage over other exchanges because of their infrastructure. Mining businesses require support from specialized lawyers, brokerage houses, geologists, accountants, and consultants. Because Toronto has arguably the best infrastructure in the world, mining companies can progress their properties. Also, they can get analyst coverage more easily than companies listed on AIM or other exchanges.

With that being said, from the point of view of an investor, the lack of coverage on AIM can be a good thing. You can develop an edge on AIM stocks because some have zero analyst coverage. By investing time studying them, you can find mispriced opportunities because other investors do not get any help from analysts. For example, you can discover AIM stocks with promising properties that are in the process of moving from AIM to the TSX in order to take advantage of the better infrastructure.

To attract small and emerging companies, AIM has a simplified regulatory environment. For example, while the LSE is regulated by the UK Financial Conduct Authority (FCA), which is an independent body funded by fees paid by the firms it regulates, AIM is self-regulated. Actually, AIM is regulated by its parent company, the LSE, which delegates the regulation primarily to nominated advisers, known as NOMADs, who are approved by the exchange.

During AIM's admission process, companies generally do not have to file a formal prospectus, but they do have to file an admission document that includes similar information. The benefit of filing an admission document instead of a prospectus is that the admission document does not require approval by the FCA, also known as the UK Listing Authority, while the prospectus does. Also, AIM does not have official underwriters in charge of due diligence. Instead, companies must appoint and hire NOMADs who walk them through the admission process. NOMADs review the company's documents and determine, on behalf of the LSE, whether a company is suitable for admission to AIM. NOMADs also provide advice and guidance to the companies they oversee so that they maintain compliance with AIM's rules.

Obviously, there is a conflict of interest because NOMADs are chosen and compensated by the listing companies, so they have an incentive to approve their clients. However, they cannot be too negligent because the LSE may take away their approved nominated adviser status. Also, investors know about AIM's relaxed regulatory environment, so some companies choose to distinguish themselves through their choice of NOMADs. For example, companies such as Merrill Lynch or Goldman Sachs can act as NOMADs.

After a successful IPO, NOMADs advise the companies on an ongoing basis throughout their public lives on AIM. For example, they help them with annual compliance reports and semi-annual updates. Note that I said semi-annual updates. AIM-listed companies do not have quarterly reporting requirements. They have semi-annual reporting requirements.

ASX

Australia is a major destination for mining companies to list their shares after Canada and the UK. Australia is the home of the Australian Securities Exchange (ASX). Unlike its competitors, the ASX does not have a separate exchange for junior exploration companies. The juniors and seniors trade alongside each other on the same board.

Of all the exchanges, the ASX is the most diverse in terms of mining and the least diverse in terms of geography. It is home to all kinds of mining companies from coal to iron ore to gold. However, the ASX is heavily dominated by Australian companies. Mining companies listed on the ASX may look for a dual listing to gain exposure to international investors.

The listing requirements on the ASX are a bit stricter in comparison to those of competing exchanges, such as the TSXV and AIM. For example, companies have to pass either a profit or asset test. With exploration companies, it comes down to an asset test since they have no profits. To pass the asset test, the candidates need to have net tangible assets of at least $3 million or a market capitalization post-IPO of at least $10 million, and working capital of at least $1.5 million. However, the ASX grants listings on a case-by-case basis and may make exceptions to the rule.

During the admission process, a prospectus is prepared. It must be approved not only by the due diligence committee, which consists of lawyers, underwriters, accountants, and consultants, but also by the board of directors. After their approval, the prospectus is lodged with the Australian Securities and Investments Commission (ASIC). After the lodgment, the prospectus must be made available to the investing public for a minimum of seven days. This is called the "exposure period." After this period is over, the listing company can start selling shares and raising money.

In terms of reporting requirements, ASX-listed entities are required to report semi-annually (like on AIM) and annually. However, exploration companies have to make additional quarterly updates about mining, exploration, and development activities, and the expenditures associated with those activities. It makes sense because investors want to know how fast cash is being burned on more than a semi-annual basis.

Private Placement

After completing a successful IPO and obtaining a concurrent listing on an official exchange, the company will have the necessary funds to work on its property. The money will be used for drilling, sampling, and other studies. The idea is to generate positive drilling and sampling results to make the property more valuable. This should cause the stock price to increase.

This allows the management to issue more shares at higher prices. However, instead of raising funds through an IPO, which has already taken place, the company can issue additional shares through private placements. Before discussing what a private placement is in detail, let's delve into what happens when a company is not able to achieve the positive results needed to ensure that investors keep forking out more money.

Delisting

Because exploration companies are hungry for capital and years away from generating any revenues, they rely on investors for survival. The moment they run out of money and there is no new capital coming, the game is over. Because of this simple fact, they have to keep stimulating their investor base with good news.

Unfortunately, no matter how hard they try, the probabilities of finding new gold discoveries are stacked against them. Most fail, run out of money, and watch helplessly as their stock prices go into free fall. At some point, they are no longer able to comply with the exchange's requirements and are delisted.

If they trade on the TSXV, they may transition to the NEX, which is referred by some investors as the "TSX graveyard." The NEX is a separate trading platform for companies that have failed to maintain a listing on the TSXV. This is a place where these companies go to figure out what to do next.

They might get acquired by other companies looking to do reverse takeovers instead of traditional IPOs. They might sell out completely if they can find an interested buyer. Or they might dissolve. Either way, the shareholders from the original IPO lose out.

If the original shares of the failed company were floated on an exchange other than the TSXV, then the shares would most likely be demoted to a "matched bargain" private trading platform. This is where a matched bargain service provider acts as a facilitator of a transaction between a buyer and seller of delisted shares. The liquidity is extremely low and the shares trade only by appointment when a seller and buyer are matched. Since these are shares of failed companies, the seller cannot expect to get a lot of money for them.

Additional Funding

If the exploration companies are successful at generating good news and instilling hope among their investors, then they can raise more money from them in the form of private placements.

Private placements are securities offerings that are exempt from registration with the SEC. They are sometimes referred to as secondary offerings. They can be done for both private and public enterprises. When done for public companies, they are referred to as "PIPE"—Private Investment in Public Equity.

Private placements are similar to public offerings and IPOs in that they issue new shares and raise capital. However, they are different because a private placement memorandum is generally issued instead of a prospectus, and the securities are usually restricted, meaning that certain conditions must be met before they can be sold to the general public.

In the US, there are several exemptions that companies can use to avoid registering offerings with the SEC. Some examples are those allowed under Section 4(a)(2) of the Securities Act of 1933 and Rules 504, 505, and 506 of Regulation D. Each exemption has its own restrictions, such as how much money can be raised and how many, if any, non-accredited investors can participate. In other countries, companies can use similar exemptions to avoid registering offerings with the respective regulatory agencies.

Requiring the registration of securities with the authorities protects investors. Exempting offerings from registration puts investors at greater risk. This is why most exemptions restrict private placement offerings to qualified or accredited investors, who, based on the country and the specific conditions, may be referred to as "sophisticated investors," "certified high net worth investors," or other similar terms.

Accredited investors include banks, insurance companies, mutual funds, and wealthy individuals.

The idea is that these investors are well informed and do not need a formal prospectus.

The types of securities that are usually sold through private placements are common shares, warrants, and flow-through shares. All of these types of shares can also be sold through public offerings as well.

Common Shares

Common shares are the same type of shares that are sold during the IPO. However, when sold through private placements, they have some restrictions. For example, holders of these shares are not allowed to sell them for a specified time period.

Because the common shares issued during the IPO trade freely on an exchange, the common shares issued through private placements have to be priced in relation to them. For example, if the common stock is trading for $1 per share, the common shares issued through the private placement cannot be priced at $3 per share. No one is dumb enough to pay $3 per share when the same share can be purchased for $1 in the open market. Actually, they might be priced slightly below at $0.80 or $0.90 per share to incentivize investors to participate.

Warrants

To lessen the impact of sale restrictions and sweeten the deal even more, companies issue warrants along with common shares. Depending on the market and the company's financial condition, they might issue either a half or full warrant with each common share purchased. The issuance of warrants does not bring any money to the company's treasury. The money is exchanged only when warrants are exercised.

A warrant is a contract between the company and an investor in which the investor has the right but not the obligation to purchase a certain number of common shares at a predetermined price. The investor usually has two to five years from the date of the private offering to exercise this right.

Warrants also have to be priced in relation to the freely trading common shares. This time, however, they are priced above the trading price. For example, if the common stock is trading for $1 per share, then the exercise price of the warrant may be $1.50 or $1.80 per share.

Mining companies issue warrants as part of private placements not only because it is traditional to do so, but also because warrants help incentivize investors to invest in the company. Without the warrants, the company might have to issue common shares at a cheaper price. However, if the market is really hot, then companies might get away without issuing warrants because the demand is so strong.

When an investor exercises a warrant, the company receives the money and issues new shares in return. So, the issuance of common shares in private placements is immediately dilutive to existing shareholders while the issuance of warrants is not. Warrants are only dilutive when they are exercised, and they might never be exercised if the stock price does not increase enough to make it worth it.

Sometimes warrants may be separated from common stock shares and trade freely on their own. Consequently, it is not uncommon for an investor to sell the common shares after the restriction period lapses and hold on to the warrants only.

There is some confusion among investors about warrants versus options because options (more specifically, call options) also give investors the right but not the obligation to purchase common shares at a predetermined price. Without getting into too much detail, the main difference between the two is that a warrant contract is between an investor and a company while an option contract is between two investors. When warrants are exercised, the companies themselves deliver the shares. When options are exercised, the other investor delivers the shares.

Flow-Through Shares

Another type of shares that can be sold through private placements is flow-through shares. They are identical to common shares except for one additional benefit. They allow Canadian exploration companies to transfer their tax deductions to Canadian investors upon meeting certain conditions. Only Canadian tax code allows them.

The Canadian government altered the tax code to help junior mining companies raise money. It makes sense since the juniors do not have revenue to deduct their expenditures against. But someone (the shareholder) is paying for all the expenses. Why not allow them to deduct it against their personal incomes? The exploration companies need all the help they can get—allowing deductions makes it easier for them to raise money because more investors find their shares more attractive.

To make it happen, the company and the investors enter into an agreement where the investors provide the capital and the company issues shares and transfers eligible exploration and development expenses to them. The companies have 24 months to spend the money on specific items, like exploration, that are outlined in the tax code; otherwise, investors do not get the deduction. The benefit to investors is obvious, but they have to hold the shares for a period of time to get the tax deductions. The companies, on the other hand, are able to raise equity capital a little bit more cheaply because they can price the flow-through shares higher.

There two types of flow-through shares that can be issued: regular and super. Regular flow-through shares allow a 100 percent deduction for eligible exploration and development expenses, while super flow-through shares allow the same plus a federal tax credit, known as the Mineral Exploration Tax Credit, equal to 15 percent of grassroots exploration expenses.

Non-Brokered Deals

To carry out private placements, companies may engage brokers or they might do it themselves. If they chose to go it alone, such private placements are called non-brokered. This is when the company's investor relations department sells the shares directly to investors.

Non-brokered deals may appeal to companies because they enable them to have more control over the selling process and allow them to avoid paying brokerage fees. Generally, existing shareholders view it more positively when their companies do non-brokered deals versus brokered deals because it demonstrates strength, a good shareholder base, and strong demand for shares. If the companies have to pay money to a broker to push shares, then something might be wrong.

With that being said, some exploration companies might not have strong investor relations departments, or the management may simply want to focus on the operations and not bother with organizing road shows or other marketing activities. In such cases, they find that engaging brokers is justifiable.

Brokered Deals

When private placements are conducted with the help of brokers, they are called brokered deals. Depending on whether brokers act as agents or buyers of offered securities, brokered deals are further divided into best efforts or bought deals.

In best efforts deals, investment banks acting as brokers do not buy the new securities, but agree to do their best to sell either all or a minimum number of them within a specified time. If the minimum number of shares does not sell, the entire offering will be withdrawn. In order to sell the new securities, the brokers call their clients, organize road shows, conduct conference calls, publish brochures, and coordinate face-to-face meetings with management. The brokers perform these activities to help the issuers accomplish their goal, which is to raise capital at the cheapest cost. For this service, the brokers are paid a commission, which is negotiated with the issuer.

While best efforts deals have many benefits for both issuers and brokers, some companies enter into bought deals. This is when the broker buys all the offered shares from the issuer and the issuer does not have to worry about anything but depositing a check at the bank. They do not have to waste their time attending road shows. They do not have to get on conference calls or go to face-to-face meetings. They can just focus on the operations. Also, they do not have to worry about other investors front running them by selling shares, because the word will get out about a private placement in the works.

Bought deals are fast. Some people call them overnight deals. The broker and issuer agree on a price right after the close of the trading day, which is 4 PM Eastern Standard Time. Then, the broker has until the beginning of the next trading day, which is 9:30 AM, to sell those shares, or he is stuck holding them. Then, he might be forced to sell them at a loss once the word is out that a bought deal is in the works. People will most likely dump their shares, causing the stock price to drop.

Obviously, the broker must get a decent discount to the closing price because he is not getting paid a commission. He makes money on the spread between what he purchases the shares for, which is usually not disclosed, and the price that he sells them for, also known as the clearing price, which is disclosed. Also, the discount has to be big enough for the buyers of these shares to also buy at a discount. Here is what I mean.

If the stock closed at $2 per share at 4 PM, the broker cannot pay $2 for the new shares. If he gets them for $1.70 per share, then he can turn around and sell them overnight to someone else for $1.85 per share, making a $0.15 margin. To incentivize the buyers, he has to offer them a discount to the current trading price; otherwise, they have no reason to buy. The buyers can simply wait until the next trading day and get the shares in the open market for the same or even a better price.

The reason why most deals are not bought deals is because they are risky for brokers, and existing shareholders hate them. Some people hate bought deals with a passion.

During bought deals, all the risk falls on the brokers. If they cannot sell the shares for prices higher than what they paid, they lose money. So, they only do them when they are absolutely sure they can complete them successfully, which means the issuers must be of high quality. They will probably not be companies in an early exploration stage. But when the issuers are popular, what is the point of doing bought deals in the first place?

Current shareholders hate bought deals for several reasons. They feel that companies are leaving money on the table by discounting the price significantly. If the broker can sell the shares overnight, then it must not be that hard to sell them in the first place. It is a slap in the face.

Another reason why shareholders hate them is because, as I said previously, they usually cause the stock price to tumble the next morning. Then, the stock price might stay depressed for quite some time. The reason for this is that some of the new buyers will sell the shares the next morning to lock in short-term profits. You might say, "But aren't they barred from selling those shares?" Yes, they are, but some of the buyers might already have shares. So, if they already have 20,000 shares and they buy 20,000 new shares, they can sell the 20,000 old shares and just keep the new shares. It is like getting free money. Also, some other buyers might short sell shares and deliver them when the selling restriction period on the newly acquired shares passes.

Brokers try to prevent that from happening by only selling to long-term shareholders. However, if they cannot find enough of them, they will settle on flippers. At the end of the day, the brokers carry all the risk, so they will do whatever it takes to unload the shares before 9:30 AM the next morning.

Bought deals also save the company the headache of doing a marketed road show. Management teams often prefer to focus on their businesses and leave the marketing to brokers. An issuer may choose a bought deal because it can be accomplished quickly. There is little possibility for investor front running. Usually, bought deals are done on higher-quality companies.

Summary

In general, exploration companies are very risky. They have no revenue, big expenses, and huge plans. Their assets do not have much value, so they cannot be monetized. Consequently, most capital providers shy away from them. Therefore, their financing and funding options are limited. At this point, all roads point to equity financing.

CHAPTER 2

Evaluation

CHAPTER 2

Evaluation

UP UNTIL THE DECISION is made to build a mine, everything about the project is evaluation and testing. Drilling is testing. Sampling is testing. Scoping is testing. Everything is testing to see if the project can eventually be brought into profitable production.

The reason gold mining companies have limited financing options during the early stages is because the uncertainty is high. How do you know if a mine can be brought into production if you don't even know the grade, the size, or the location of the deposit? As a result, the people that take the gamble at an early stage are the founders, friends of the founders, and speculators. They are the people that provide equity financing.

However, as more information is obtained about the projects through various studies, the certainty of future production increases, and more and more financing opportunities open up. Examples of evaluation studies include scoping studies, preliminary economic studies, and detailed feasibility studies.

The goal of most exploration companies is not to put their projects into production, but to find and evaluate gold deposits. This way, they become interesting and valuable to cash-rich mining companies looking to acquire deposits to replenish their depleting production.

Usually, in order for exploration companies to prove there is value in their projects, they need to have an NI 43-101 technical report completed and a PEA (Preliminary Economic Assessment) performed. This gives potential acquirers something concrete to base their analyses on. Remember, these companies are not gamblers. They make fundamentally oriented acquisition decisions.

An NI 43-101 is a technical report that primarily describes the size and quality (meaning grade) of the deposit. In order for a third-party engineering firm to complete such a report, it needs lots of drilling data and sample results from the company. Gathering that data costs money, and this is primarily what the funds raised through the IPO and private placements were supposed to be spent on.

If the company raised enough money during the early financing rounds, then it might still have enough to pay for the NI 43-101. It might even have enough to do the PEA. However, if it does not, then it needs to raise more money.

Assuming that the drilling results are promising, the company might not only tap into equity financing but also alternative financing.

Alternative Financing

Progressing projects from exploration to production is like putting money down a very deep hole. When the company finally attracts other forms of financing, equity holders can take a little breather. The alternative types of financing available at this stage may include royalty, earn-in, and joint venture agreements.

Royalty

Under royalty financing, a company enters into an agreement with a capital provider, usually a specialty royalty company, where it receives a one-time, lump-sum payment to finance exploration or mine construction in return for a percentage of revenues over the life of the mine, commonly called life-of-mine (LOM). Because there are no new shares being issued, there is no dilution to existing shareholders. However, the company getting the money is giving up some upside because a royalty means giving up a percentage of something in the future.

Note that a royalty company does not make a dime until the property it finances is in production. Consequently, royalty companies perform their due diligence thoroughly before they go ahead with any deal. There is no hard rule, but they typically do not get involved until the company can demonstrate indicated reserves through a drilling program. It makes sense because the indicated reserves classification gives them some confidence as to the size and quality of a deposit and how it will translate into royalty payments.

There are numerous types of royalties, and they are usually based on either future revenues or profits. In this section, I will cover the three most common types of royalties. However, you should know that in practice, each royalty agreement is custom made and spells out details such as how many ounces must be produced before the royalty becomes payable and which costs are to be deducted before calculating the royalty payment.

The three most common types of royalties are:
- Gross Royalty (GR)
- Net Smelter Return Royalty (NSR)
- Net Profits Interest (NPI)

A gross royalty is based on a percentage of gross revenue produced by the mine. Usually, no deductions are made before the royalty is calculated. Gross royalties can be burdensome on mine operators because they must be paid regardless of whether the mine is profitable. They often range from 1 to 5 percent. In the example that follows, I will assume that the royalty is being calculated based on the spot price for gold with no deduction for smelting and refining costs.

Example:

Royalty rate = 2 percent
Gold price = $1,150 per ounce
Refining Costs = $20 per ounce
Cash costs = $800 per ounce
Transportation and insurance = $10 per ounce

Gross Royalty	=	X Percent	x	Gold Price
	=	2%	x	$1,150
Gross Royalty	=	$23.00		

A net smelter return royalty is a percentage of the gross revenue produced by the mine, less deductions for off-mine costs, such as transportation, insurance, smelting, and refining, in the event that they were not already deducted by the purchaser when calculating the payment. No deductions are made for production and operating costs, which are typically referred to as cash costs. The term net smelter return refers to the proceeds the mine operator receives from the sale of its impure gold product to the smelter or refinery. Net smelter return royalties typically range from 1 to 4 percent.

Net Smelter Return Royalty	=	X Percent	x	Gold Price	-	Refining Cost	-	Transportation & Insurance
	=	2%	x	$1,150	-	$20	-	$10
	=	2%	x	$1,120				
NSR	=	$22.40						

A net profits interest royalty is a percentage of the net profit, which includes deductions related to operating and production costs, or cash costs. This type of royalty typically does not become payable until the operating and production costs have been covered and the miner has recouped the pre-production expenditures and capital costs it incurred while building the mine. Net profits interest royalties are typically around 3 to 10 percent.

Net Profits Interest Royalty	=	X%	x	Gold Price	-	Refining Cost	-	Trans. & Insurance	-	Cash Costs
	=	10%	x	$1,150	-	$20	-	$10	-	$800
	=	10%	x	$320						
NPI	=	$32.00								

Out of all the royalty types, the net smelter return royalty is the most popular. It is the easiest to implement and monitor. Different parties have different opinions about which royalties are the fairest. For example, the mining companies prefer royalties to be based on profitability. This means that a net profits interest royalty is the most appealing to them because it takes cash costs into account, and they are only required to pay a royalty when the production is profitable.

The royalty companies, on the other hand, do not favor net royalties because they know that miners can easily manipulate and inflate expenses. Some in the industry cynically call it the "no payment intended" royalty. Therefore, they do not want to allow operating expenses to be deducted before royalties are calculated. Consequently, they favor gross royalties or net smelter return royalties, which do not permit the deduction of operating costs. These types of royalties ensure that they will get paid. But, if the underlying operation is not profitable in the long term, the royalty companies will not get paid because the mine will shut down. In some cases, a gross royalty could be so burdensome that it could actually be the cause of a mine shutting down.

As mentioned before, royalty financing is beneficial to gold companies because it provides them with capital without diluting shareholders. Also, it brings in patient money because royalty companies, unlike bankers, understand the mining business. They know that this is a tough business. This is why they chose to be in the royalty financing business in the first place—to avoid dealing with all the headaches of delays and cost overruns. Therefore, they are more understanding and usually supply capital with no covenants. But because they are patient, once in production, they usually stay with the miner for the entire life-of-mine. Depending on the agreement, they may allow the miner to buy them out with cash or equity in the future.

The amount of money that gold companies can raise through royalty financing is usually on the low end. This means that the proceeds are more likely to be used for progressing properties through drilling programs towards the pre-feasibility or feasibility studies rather than financing the mine development.

Let's say that the property has 1 million gold ounces in the ground with a 10-year life-of-mine. This would equate to a potential production of 100,000 ounces per year. If we used the same variables as before, the royalty company would make the following amount over the life-of-mine.

Net smelter return royalty = 2 percent x ($1,150 - $20 Refining Cost - $10 Transportation and Insurance) = $22.40 per ounce

100,000 ounces per year x $22.40 per ounce = $2,240,000 per year

10 years x $2,240,000 = $22,400,000

So, if the royalty company expects to collect $22.4 million over the life-of-mine, it would not supply the company more than $22.4 million because it would not make any money. It would have to supply maybe $10 to $15 million in a lump sum to collect $22.4

million over 10 years for the transaction to be worth it.

Earn-In and Joint Venture

When advancing projects, junior mining companies can do it alone or they can bring in partners by forming joint ventures with larger mining companies or financial investors. When they work with larger mining companies, which is usually the case, the partners bring money and technical expertise to the table, and the exploration companies bring properties. Successful joint ventures can be beneficial for both parties. The junior gets to advance its project without issuing more shares while the senior gets part of a property to help replenish its diminishing production. The greatest disadvantage to the junior is that it usually loses operational control.

Note that even though the explorer does not print more shares, dilution still takes place. However, instead of the dilution being at the corporate level, it happens at the asset level because at the end of the day, the shareholders end up owning a smaller percentage of the asset.

Like royalty companies, joint venture partners can enter the picture at any time during the property's development cycle, but they usually need to see some value before they will consider doing a deal. Just like royalty companies, they are fundamentalists. They want to see ounces that they can put into production.

In order to obtain a percentage of an exploration property, joint venture partners can either pay for it up front or they can earn an interest by performing various tasks outlined in the agreement. For example, the senior might be required to spend $5 million on exploration drilling to earn a 25 percent interest in the property. They may also have the option of spending an additional $5 million in order to earn up to 50 percent. There are no rules regarding how they can get their piece. Everything is negotiable.

 While joint ventures and earn-in agreements have their advantages, they can also create lots of conflicts between the parties, causing them to butt heads. This is because the juniors and the seniors have completely different agendas.

At the beginning, the juniors want the seniors to come in, spend money, get the work done, and earn their interests as fast as possible. This is what generates excitement among the junior's shareholders. They want the stock price to get moving. If they do not want to spend, they should get out of the way.

The seniors, on the other hand, could not care less about the junior's stock price. They want to take their sweet time and have the option to walk away. They have several other properties—some in production, some in advanced stages, and some in the process of being acquired. They also have their own shareholders to worry about, and they want to show them that they are good stewards of capital.

Consequently, they want to prioritize and start spending money on the junior's property when it is convenient for them. Their goal is to build a pipeline of projects in various stages of production and development and the junior's project is just one piece of the puzzle in their entire master plan.

Because of this, the juniors do not want to give the seniors any ownership until they start spending money, but the seniors do not want to spend any money until they know they own some of the property already. They want their interest to vest immediately upon signing a joint venture agreement. It is a Catch-22.

When the seniors finally get around to working for their ownership share, there are more problems that can come up. The juniors do not want the seniors to waste money on unnecessary (in their opinion) items because if the seniors overspend, they might earn their interests too soon without too much to show for it. Then, the juniors end up losing a bigger chunk of the property when additional money is spent.

The seniors, on the other hand, are not gamblers. When they do something, they want to get it right the first time. They tend to do most of the work up front so that there are few surprises later on. They do not think that doing extensive preparatory work is wasteful.

One other item that infuriates juniors is that seniors want to allocate a percentage of their fixed corporate costs toward their project. This can quickly add up without any advancement of the subject property.

In the later stages, meaning after the seniors finally earn their interests, they do not want to be delayed and bothered by the smaller partner. That is why they seek full operational control. Once they decide to advance the project, they want to advance it. They want to build a mine. The problem is that in a joint venture, both parties are usually responsible for their pro rata share of development costs after the initial earn-in. Well, the juniors are always broke and the seniors want to get moving. They do not want to wait for the junior to raise money so that it can pony up its portion. The junior, on the other hand, wants to take the time needed to raise its portion so that its interest in the asset is not diluted by the senior's ability to outspend it.

As you can see, there are lots of problems that can come up during joint ventures. In order to minimize such conflicts and reap the benefits of joint ventures, the responsibilities of both parties should be clearly spelled out in the agreements. Nothing should be omitted and taken for granted. Resulting delays and lawsuits are expensive and distracting.

Equity Crowdfunding

During the stage when exploration companies have something to show in terms of drilling results and various studies, they can start attracting other sources of financing. However, at any stage, equity financing is always available as long as investors are willing to write checks.

After President Obama signed the Jumpstart Our Business Startups (JOBS) Act into law in April 2012, another equity funding option became available to small companies—crowdfunding. As the name implies, crowdfunding is a way to raise capital by soliciting small amounts of money from large numbers of individuals, usually via crowdfunding websites, but sometimes via social media sites like Facebook or Twitter. The main goal of the act was to help small businesses access capital more easily.

Any company in the United States that wants to raise funding by selling securities must either register its securities offering with the SEC or qualify for an exemption from registration. Registering a securities offering with the SEC makes a company a public company. The traditional exemption has been Rule 506(b) under Regulation D. As part of the JOBS Act, two new exemptions were created to allow businesses to use crowdfunding to sell equity. Prior to this act, crowdfunding could not be used to sell securities in the United States.

One exemption, Rule 506(c), lifts the ban on the mass marketing of private securities offerings, and the other, called the Regulation Crowdfunding exemption, allows non-accredited individuals to invest in private companies. Both exemptions are subject to several conditions.

Several other countries have also passed legislation to regulate crowd-sourced equity funding. In Canada, securities regulation is handled at the provincial level, and several provinces have created similar exemptions, such as an exemption from filing a prospectus. In the UK, the Financial Conduct Authority (FCA) regulates crowdfunding activities by requiring crowdfunding platforms to be authorized and to screen for non-sophisticated investors, who are only allowed to invest up to a certain amount. Smaller offerings are exempt from preparing prospectuses, and some marketing restrictions apply. As of the writing of this book, crowd-sourced funding legislation has been proposed in the Australian parliament, but has not yet been passed.

Crowdfunding is a new way for mining companies to access capital that can be used to supplement other financing options. Also, during times when capital is really difficult to raise, crowdfunding can put the companies in the driver's seat when it comes to financing their projects.

In 2013, ExplorationFunder, the first crowdfunding platform designed to cater to early-stage companies in the natural resource sector, was launched. However, the website, Explorationfunder.com, is no longer active.

At this point, crowdfunding, especially for mineral exploration, is just in its early stages, but it is gaining traction because the mining industry is desperate for capital. Even PDAC (Prospectors and Developers Association of Canada) is looking for a way to introduce crowdfunding into its offerings.

The website Mineralintelligence.com is a global registry of mining projects that are seeking investment. It was launched in 2015 at a time when the Australian government was expected to pass new legislation to allow equity crowdfunding. The founders planned to offer equity crowdfunding services, but the bill faced delays, and the site launched with a focus on listing for-sale mining projects and connecting them with a subscriber base. The company is already offering some crowdfunding opportunities for mining companies through equity crowdfunding platform Equitise in New Zealand, where legislation has already been passed to allow and regulate crowdfunding. Once similar legislation finally passes in Australia, the company will be ready to take advantage of it.

Red Cloud Klondike Strike (Klondikestrike.com) was launched in March 2016 in Canada as the first equity crowdfunding platform to focus solely on mining. The company also wants to use crowdfunding to offer other types of financing options, such as bridge loans, flow-through shares, streaming agreements, and royalty deals. They also want to branch out into property transactions.

Primarybid.com is a crowdfunding platform specifically for AIM-listed companies; however, it is a little different because it allows private investors to bid for new shares. Once a certain threshold is reached, companies can choose whether to accept the bids and issue new shares. The site went live in beta form in March 2015 and was formally launched in March 2016. It has raised money for ten companies as of the writing of this book. Seven are in the natural resource sector, and of those, two are gold mining companies.

With that being said, crowdfunding has the potential to really change the way mining companies raise money. At this point, the financing transactions tend to be on the small side—$1 to $2 million. The largest deal to date that I can recall was for $12 million.

Summary

During the evaluation stage, exploration companies are trying to prove that their assets are suitable for commercial production. This requires raising capital to finance drilling exploration and various studies, such as an NI 43-101 technical report, a PEA, and feasibility studies.

Once they successfully show that their projects are worth developing, they usually sell them, unless they entered into a joint venture agreement, which may keep them involved longer. The reason why they sell is because they are experts in finding gold, not in building and operating mines. They can now take the money and start another exploration company.

CHAPTER 3

Development

Development

THE DEVELOPMENT or construction stage is the last step before production. It is also the most expensive step. Most discoveries do not make it this far because they are not economically feasible for all sorts of reasons. To reach the point when a project is given a green light for mine development, the company needs to prove in detail how it will make money. This means that the project needs to have a feasibility study with favorable results.

A feasibility study includes information such as a design for the mine, a detailed process flow sheet, projected recoveries, capital and operating cost estimates, and an economic model of the project. With this study, a lot of uncertainties are removed, and therefore, more financing options open up. This is the first time that debt financing is entertained.

Alternative Financing

Before discussing debt financing, there is one alternative financing option that was not discussed in the previous chapter—streaming. You already learned that exploration companies can use royalty, earn-in and joint venture financing options to advance their projects.

The companies that do royalty deals usually also do streaming deals. The most popular mineral royalty and streaming companies include Franco-Nevada, Royal Gold, Anglo Pacific Group, Sandstorm Gold, and Silver Wheaton. They all offer these two types of financing options. Silver Wheaton is known for having pioneered streaming in the mining sector in 2004.

People tend to confuse royalty and streaming agreements. Royalty financing transactions involve a one-time payment in return for royalty payments over many years. Streaming transactions involve an up-front payment and follow-up payments in return for product delivery over many years.

Also, royalty deals tend to be smaller and used more often for the evaluation of gold deposits while streaming deals tend to be larger and used for mine construction. The reason why streaming is covered in this chapter and not the previous chapter is because companies typically enter into streaming transactions to build mines.

In a streaming transaction, a capital provider enters into an agreement with the mining company to buy a portion of its future production at a predetermined price. For example, the agreement might say that the streaming company will buy 30,000 gold ounces per year for nine years for $700 per ounce, and the price of gold is $1,200 per ounce at the time of the agreement.

For this right, the streaming company makes an up-front payment that is used to build a mine. Then, when the mine is producing, the streamer pays the miner $700 for every ounce of gold delivered.

In this example, the streaming company would make $135 million over nine years on the difference between the market price of $1,200 per ounce and the predetermined price of $700 per ounce. This, of course, assumes the price of gold stays at $1,200 per ounce.

$135 million = 30,000 ounces x ($1,200 - $700) x 9 years

In exchange for such an income stream, the streamer could afford to make an up-front payment of $70 or $80 million to the miner, which is significantly more than a typical royalty deal.

A streaming deal can be done not only for the production of gold, but also for the production of a by-product, such as silver. As you know, there is always some amount of by-product produced during gold production. Mining companies use the sale of a by-product as a credit toward the overall cost to produce the core product. Streaming deals might involve only the sale or the streaming of the by-product instead of the core product.

As you can see, the streaming company only makes money when it buys the metal produced for less than the market price. However, selling the product for too little is the biggest risk the mining company faces. The predetermined price cannot be too low, and the agreement cannot ask for too many ounces in relation to total production. If the agreement puts too much strain on the miner, then it is not sustainable and everybody loses. It has to be a win-win for both parties.

For example, if the project produces gold for $900 per ounce, it would probably not be too smart to set the predetermined price at $600 per ounce because the miner would be losing serious money on each ounce delivered to the streamer. Also, if the project is capable of producing 100,000 ounces per year, it would be too risky to sell 90,000 ounces per year through a streaming deal. The mining company would have very little left for itself. Consequently, both parties have to really look at the economics of the underlying project and structure streaming agreements accordingly.

For these reasons, some projects are rejected by streaming companies because there needs to be enough room in their economics for everybody to make money. Streaming companies prefer low-cost producers. This ensures that the mining companies still make money even after selling their product at a discount to the market price. Also, streamers shy away from overstreaming. Some will not take the deal if more than 20 percent of production is streamed.

In general, mining companies like streaming deals because they are cheaper than equity and safer than debt. Like royalties, the streaming transactions bring in patient money with knowledge of the mining business. Streaming companies, on the other hand, like streaming because they get to be involved in the mining business without exposure to rising costs. They get to buy the product at fixed prices and benefit from an increase in the gold price. In other words, they are leveraged to the increasing price of gold and somewhat protected from a decrease in the price of gold.

Forward Sales

Another alternative financing option that mine developers can use is the forward gold sales agreement. Under this type of agreement, a mining company receives an up-front payment in return for agreeing to sell all or some of its production in the future at a predetermined price and date. You might say that this sounds exactly like streaming. Well, it is almost identical except for one main difference—a predetermined date.

Under a streaming agreement, the miner does not have to deliver gold until it achieves production. If production is delayed, so is the delivery of the product. Remember, streamers understand that mining is prone to delays.

With a forward sales contract, the miner has to deliver the product according to a pre-planned schedule whether the mine is producing or not. Consequently, these contracts can be pretty risky if the other side is inflexible.

For example, in August 2011, Yukon-Nevada Gold (now Veris Gold) and Deutsche Bank entered into a $120 million forward sales agreement. In February 2012, the two parties entered into a second forward sales agreement for $20 million. So, in total, the mining company raised $140 million to improve its processing facility. In return, the company was obligated to deliver to Deutsche Bank a little more than 200,000 gold ounces over 48 months at a price of approximately $800 per ounce. The first deal was struck when the price of gold was $1,800 per ounce.

The shareholders were celebrating the capital raise, especially the first one for $120 million, because the company was able to raise a lot of money without diluting them. Little did they know that this deal was going to force the company into bankruptcy a few years later.

The problem was that the repayment of the forward gold sales agreement had a certain schedule as shown in the following graph.

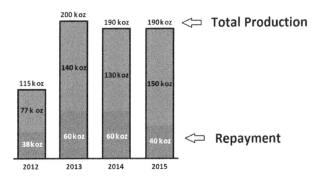

In 2012, the company had to deliver 38,000 gold ounces to Deutsche Bank. By 2013, the repayment amount jumped to 60,000 ounces. This was not supposed to be a problem because by then, the company was going to produce 200,000 ounces per year.

Unfortunately, Yukon-Nevada kept running into all sorts of operational problems, and by 2013, it was barely able to produce 150,000 ounces of gold. Also, because the price of gold collapsed, the entire production was unprofitable.

This did not matter to Deutsche Bank, which wanted its 60,000 ounces per year no matter what. As a result, the company was getting suffocated every month. It tried to renegotiate the terms with the bank with no success. Finally, in June 2014, the company could not take it anymore and filed for bankruptcy protection.

Looking back, the management should have raised $140 million by printing new shares and diluting shareholders instead of entering into a forward gold sales agreement. If the company did that, then there would have been no bankruptcy. With that being said, hindsight is 20/20.

What you should take away from this example is that forward gold sales agreements are another form of alternative financing. They look almost identical to streaming agreements, but they are significantly more risky because of their inflexible repayment schedules.

Debt

Upon successful results from the feasibility study, a company might be able to qualify for debt financing for the construction of a mine and processing facility. Such a loan is usually in the form of project financing backed by some or all of the company's assets.

Even though by that time, a lot of uncertainties have been removed regarding the economics of the project, the construction stage is risky because a lot of things can go wrong, and the debt provider is usually a bank or some other financial institution that is not flexible and understanding. Bankers are known to be risk averse, and they have no problem calling the loans when problems appear. Also, project financing requires significantly more money than any work that has already been done on the project so mistakes are magnified. The construction cost figures run into hundreds of millions of dollars versus the tens of millions spent in earlier stages. Consequently, when the loans cannot be repaid and serviced from profitable gold production, the company must issue more shares—now with a plunging stock price—to pay off the bankers. This severely dilutes existing shareholders.

For example, Midway Gold borrowed $55 million from the Commonwealth Bank of Australia to finance the development of the Pan gold mine in White Pine County, Nevada. It also borrowed another $70 million in preferred shares, which are essentially debt. Upon the completion of the mine, the company learned that the grade of the deposit was not as high as it originally estimated. Consequently, the mine production was not profitable, but the loans still had to be paid back. When I started writing this book, the stock price collapsed to levels where the company's market cap was only $15 million. If the shareholders would have come up with money in the form of equity to rescue their company by paying off the debt, the dilution would have been almost 1,000 percent. However, if the mine development was financed with equity in the first place, then the dilution would have been a lot smaller because at that time, the stock price was 10 times higher. Eventually, the company went bankrupt and investors lost everything.

Even though debt financing can be risky since things can go wrong, it is a common way to finance the development of mining projects because it is a way to raise large sums of money cheaply. The interest rates are only 300 to 400 basis points higher than LIBOR. After the construction of a mine is complete and it is successfully producing gold like it is supposed to according to the feasibility study, then shareholders can make a lot of money.

Project facility loans usually consists of two tranches: a project facility (PF) and a cost overrun facility (COF). The project facility portion is the main part of the loan and carries a lower interest rate while the cost overrun facility carries a higher interest rate and may equal only 20 percent of the project facility. For example, Midway Gold's loan was for a total of $55 million, of which $45 million was the project facility and $10 million was the cost overrun facility.

Because it takes months and even years to complete the construction, the company receives the money in stages when certain milestones are reached. As with everything else, details like this are negotiated. Also, the time when the loan payments start is also negotiated. For a specific time frame, both parties rely on the feasibility study, which estimates the construction period.

As you know, commodity prices can swing widely in either direction. This volatility creates concern among bankers because unfavorable movement in the gold price can cause a mining project to be unable to service its debt. Consequently, debt facility providers might require gold companies to hedge their production at a fixed price to ensure the ability to repay. In order to hedge their production, the miner would enter into a forward sales agreement with the bank or another party to sell all or a portion of its future gold production at a fixed price. In this case, the forward sales agreement would not have an up-front payment from the other party because the predetermined price would be somewhere around the current market price. For example, in order for Midway Gold to get the loan from Commonwealth, it was required to hedge 80,500 ounces of gold over a 23-month period at $1,200 per ounce.

Equipment Financing

When construction figures are presented in feasibility studies, they include the cost of mining equipment, such as haul trucks. Sometimes, the project facility is large enough to cover the cost of mining equipment, and sometimes, it is not.

If there is enough money, then mining companies can purchase equipment straight from the manufacturers. If not, they can either lease it or arrange for equipment financing with the manufacturers. For example, Caterpillar, through Cat Mining Finance, assists companies in leasing and financing mining equipment.

However, leasing and outright purchase are not the only options. It is not unusual for miners to hire a mining contractor that supplies both the equipment and labor. This is the route that Midway Gold took with the Pan project. Instead of spending $30 million on its own mining equipment, it hired Ledcor to be the mining contractor.

As with everything else, there are costs and benefits. The benefits of going with a contractor are obvious. It reduces capital expenditures and the need for a miner to hire its own employees. The drawback is that it costs more to mine because the contractor needs to make a profit. For example, Midway's feasibility study estimated the mining cost to be $1 per ton, but with a contract miner, it cost the company $2 per ton.

Even with higher operating costs, there are many companies that take this route because it causes fewer headaches. Contract miners are already experts in mining, and they do not need to train a brand new workforce.

Summary

The development or construction stage is reached after lots of studies have been done on the projects. This the last step before production, which is the ultimate goal. Because various studies remove many uncertainties, more financing options open up. Then, it is up to the management to choose the most appropriate financing vehicle to get the job done and benefit the shareholders in the most rewarding way.

While it is great that so many different parties are interested in throwing money at projects in this stage, their eagerness does not mean that all risk is gone. This could not be further from the truth. Studies are only estimations. Eventually, they have to be proven right in the real world. Because development financing involves such large sums of money, projects that cannot deliver as promised can break their companies. A perfect example is Midway Gold, which had great promise. But the actual project failed in action and bankrupted the entire company.

CHAPTER 4

Production

CHAPTER 4

Production

MINING COMPANIES with profitably producing assets are the envy of all other companies in the industry. This is because once they start generating cash flow, all of a sudden, everybody wants to finance them. It is similar to how if you are rich, you can get a loan from a bank easily, but if you are poor and need the money, you cannot get it.

You might wonder, "If a mining company achieved its goal of putting its property into production, why should it raise more money?" The answer is to keep creating value. Yes, it could stop, meaning that it could just operate the mine, service the debt that financed the project, and eventually deplete the resource. But this is not how it works when you are a public company. You have to keep growing; otherwise you must sell your assets, return money to investors, and close up shop. With a producing mine, a company can really accelerate growth.

Cash Flow

The best form of financing is internally generated funds, or cash flows. If a property is producing 100,000 ounces of gold per year at a cash cost of $800 per ounce while the price of gold is $1,200 per ounce, it is earning $40 million per year. After servicing the debt and covering SG&A and other expenses, the company might have $20 or $30 million left for itself. This is serious money that can create a lot of value if allocated properly.

The cash flow can be used to expand production, make operations more efficient, increase resources and the life-of-mine, or diversify the portfolio of assets. All of these options create value for shareholders.

While being in production is a fantastic achievement, the market does not assign high valuations to single-asset mining companies, especially when they still carry project debt. This is understandable. If something goes wrong, the cash flow disappears, but the debt remains. Consequently, many mining companies want to get other projects going.

They can go back to the AIM and TSXV exchanges and look for promising assets. They can take the approach of buying properties that have already had PEAs completed with promising results, or they can be more adventurous and go for earlier-stage projects. Maybe they will choose to shop for failed projects on the NEX or matched bargain platforms. Projects don't necessarily fail because they are worthless. During bear markets when financing dries up, projects can fail because they have no one to finance them. Mining companies with cash flow can take advantage of that and build a pipeline of projects on the cheap.

Equity

Gold-producing companies can also use equity financing if their cash flow generation is not high enough to satisfy their growth plans. While cash flow in itself might not be enough, the fact that it exists allows companies to raise significant amounts of money. The same thing applies in our personal lives—$2,000 per month of cash flow will not buy you a house, but it will give you the ability to raise $350,000 through a mortgage to buy that house.

This time, however, the equity-raising opportunities are larger. In the early stages, exploration companies do not have revenues or profits and their properties are speculative. Consequently, they can only qualify for listings on venture exchanges, such as the TSXV in Canada and AIM in London. This limits how much they can raise because serious institutional money is usually not allowed to finance or trade such companies.

As these explorers develop their properties and put them into production, everything changes. Finally, they start meeting the listing requirements of larger and more prestigious exchanges. So, they uplist from the TSXV to the TSX or from AIM to the LSE. Others do dual listings and some even qualify for the NASDAQ or NYSE. They can uplist when they are in production or when their assets are advanced enough to qualify for higher exchanges.

News that a mining company has uplisted to a higher exchange is a reason to celebrate. It provides validation, greater exposure, and access to deep-pocketed capital providers. Mining companies can raise significantly more money from institutional players that are now allowed to participate in their growth. Uplisting also provides better liquidity (buying and selling of shares is easier) and a higher valuation. Because the shares are trading for more money, the management can use them as currency to acquire other projects.

For example, Timmins Gold was founded by Arturo Bonillas, president, and Bruce Bragagnolo, former CEO, in 2005. They took it public in 2006 on the TSXV. In total, they raised $3,150,000 in their initial public offering. They used part of these funds to purchase 50 percent of the San Francisco mine in the state of Sonora, Mexico, and conduct a drilling program. Later on, they acquired the remaining 50 percent of the property. Within the two years that followed, they completed a pre-feasibility study and construction of the mine. In 2010, the San Francisco mine was in commercial production and producing gold profitably.

Once the company became a gold producer, it was able to graduate from the TSXV. In March 2011, it uplisted to the TSX, and in November 2011, it obtained a second listing on what is now the NYSE MKT, formerly the NYSE Amex. Today, the shares are still trading on these two exchanges with the ticker symbols TMM on the TSX and TGD on the NYSE MKT. This is a perfect example of a successful project going from development to production.

After the company became a profitable producer, it received a higher valuation than it previously had as a non-producer. However, because it was a single-asset producer, investors kept pressuring it to do more. In 2015, the management used the company's shares as currency to acquire two large and promising assets: Caballo Blanco, which has since been sold, and Ana Paula. When Ana Paula is in commercial production, Timmins will transition from being a 100,000-ounce producer to a 200,000-ounce producer and from being a one-project company to a two-project company. By that time, the valuation could reach $1 billion, and it is mind-boggling to think that it all started in 2006 with only $3 million of IPO money. This just shows you what is possible in mining when capital is accessible and successfully allocated to advance exploration projects into commercial successes. If it wasn't for leveraging the cash flow from the San Francisco mine, these two acquisitions would never have been possible. Without cash flow, there would have been no uplisting and no currency (stock shares) to make these acquisitions.

Debt

In the previous chapter, you saw how developers can use debt to finance the construction of mines and processing facilities. This kind of debt is referred to as project debt. When they prove, through feasibility studies, that other projects are worth developing into producing mines, they can use debt financing again. Actually, the second time, it is easier to qualify because the management already has a successful track record.

With that being said, project debt financing is classified as private debt, meaning that it cannot be traded on an exchange. The debt holder can sell the private debt because it is an asset, but it has to do it through a private transaction. The fact that the debt is private and tied to an asset limits the amount of money that can be raised.

When mining companies become large by having several producing properties, they can qualify for debt at the corporate level, not just the asset level. They can raise capital by selling corporate bonds, which, just like public stocks, trade on organized exchanges.

With bond offerings, the capital raised can be in the billions. For example, on April 29, 2013, Barrick

Gold raised $3 billion in a bond offering. Obviously, with this kind of money, mining companies can buy not only projects, but also entire companies. In 2011, Barrick acquired Equinox Minerals for $7.65 billion.

So, this is what the big miners can do, but this does not mean that they should go out and raise unlimited amounts of money. The problem is that debt, like any debt, can hurt when it is taken on at the wrong time. For example, Barrick went all out when it came to debt. From 2007 to 2011, the company increased its debt from $3 billion to $13 billion. After the price of gold collapsed from $1,900 to $1,200 per ounce, the debt service for Barrick became an issue. Consequently, the company's shareholders ended up paying the price. The excess debt caused the stock to suffer much more than it would have if it only had to contend with the extreme drop in the price of gold.

Because of the risks that debt brings, some companies simply shy away from it even though they can qualify. For example, Monument Mining's CEO, Robert Baldock, does not want to use debt to grow his company despite the fact that it is a gold producer. Instead, he finances the growth mostly with equity, which infuriated shareholders when the price of gold was higher. But now, the company is still around while many others are not.

Alternative Financing

Producers can also tap into alternative financing options. They can take part of their gold production and sell it forward through forward gold sales or streaming agreements. This time, however, they would probably get better terms because much of the uncertainty and risk have been reduced. Everybody knows what the mine produces and at what cost. The figures are facts, not estimates anymore. The same thing applies to royalty transactions. If the producers want to enter into royalty agreements on a producing mine, they can.

In terms of joint ventures, they could sell a percentage of a mine and use the sale proceeds to acquire other projects. Or they can now be the dominant player in a joint venture with another junior looking to advance an exploration project.

Summary

Profitable gold producers have many options when it comes to raising additional capital and growing. I stress the word "profitable" because this makes all the difference. In March 2015, Midway Gold became a gold producer, but because of prior mistakes, its production was unprofitable. As a result, the company found itself in a terrible position for raising money. Its equity valuation had collapsed 75 percent in the span of just a few weeks. Debt covenants were violated. Bankers wanted their money back. Who wants to finance a gold producer with a failed operation?

However, if Midway Gold had been able to produce gold profitably like it was supposed to according to the feasibility studies, then the situation would have been completely different. The cash flow would have been enough to service the debt. Equity valuation would have been high. New capital providers would have been knocking on their doors to provide more capital for other projects. Unfortunately, this was not the case, and at the end of the day, the common shareholders ended up losing everything.

Conclusion

Conclusion

THROUGHOUT THIS BOOK, you learned about how gold exploration, development, and production companies can raise money to grow. As an investor in such companies, you need to understand this because without capital, they go nowhere. Everything that goes into advancing gold properties costs a lot of money.

If you are an investor in an exploration company that has no chance of raising capital, how do you expect not to lose your shirt? Well, you can hope that some miracle will advance its projects, but this is not the best way to go about it. I believe that a better way is to learn the financing side of the business and understand the financing options that gold companies have when it comes to raising funds. This will increase your chances of investment success.

Other Books Written by this Author

Other Books Written by this Author

THE FOLLOWING IS a list of books written by Mariusz Skonieczny:

- *Gold Production from Beginning to End*
- *Why Are We So Clueless about the Stock Market?*
- *The Basics of Understanding Financial Statements*
- *100 Ways to Find Investment Ideas*
- *Due Diligence: How to Research a Stock*
- *Scuttlebutt Investor*
- *Investment Wisdom*

Works Cited

Works Cited

"About the FCA." *FCA*. FCA, 20 April 2016. Web. 2 August 2016.

"AIM Factsheet, June 2016." *London Stock Exchange Group*. London Stock Exchange plc., June 2016. Web. 31 July 2016.

"AIM: FAQs." *London Stock Exchange*. London Stock Exchange plc., n.d. Web. 2 August 2016.

"AIM Regulation." *London Stock Exchange*. London Stock Exchange plc., n.d. Web. 3 August 2016.

"AIM Rules for Companies." *London Stock Exchange*. London Stock Exchange Group plc., 3 July 2016. Web. 31 July 2016.

"AIM Rules for Nominated Advisers." *London Stock Exchange*. London Stock Exchange Group plc., 3 July 2016. Web. 31 July 2016.

"AIM's Regulatory Landscape: Nominated Advisers." *London Stock Exchange*. London Stock Exchange plc., n.d. Web. 31 July 2016.

Alois, JD. "Equity Crowdfunding Site ExplorationFunder Launches Platform for Natural Resource Companies." *Crowdfund Insider*. Crowded Media Group, 6 March 2013. Web. 16 November 2016.

"ASC Notice of ASC Rule 45-517 Prospectus Exemption for Start-Up Businesses." *ASC*. Alberta Securities Commission, 26 July 2016. Web. 16 November 2016.

"ASX Listing Rules, Chapter 1 – Admission." *ASX*. ASX Limited, 8 September 2015. Web. 11 September 2016.

"Backgrounder – Mineral Exploration Tax Credit for Flow-Through Share Investors." *Department of Finance Canada*. Government of Canada, 1 March 2015. Web. 8 September 2016.

Barnett, Chance. "Why Title III of the JOBS Act Will Disappoint Entrepreneurs.'" *Forbes*. Forbes Media LLC, 13 May 2016. Web. 20 August 2016.

Brummer, Chris, and Daniel Gorfine. "The JOBS Act Isn't All 'Crowdfunding.'" *Forbes*. Forbes Media LLC, 8 October 2013. Web. 21 August 2016.

"Capital Pool Company (CPC) Program." *TMX*. TSX Inc., n.d. Web. 3 August 2016.

Carpentier, Cécile, and Jean-Marc Suret. "How Useful is Venture Capital? Evidence from Capital Pool Companies." *Laval University School of Accountancy*. Laval University, 12 September 2003. Web. 3 August 2016.

"Companies and Advisers: Nominated Advisers." *London Stock Exchange*. London Stock Exchange plc., n.d. Web. 31 July 2016.

"Corporations Amendment (Crowd-Sourced Funding) Bill 2015." *Parliament of Australia*. Parliament of Australia, n.d. Web. 16 November 2016.

"Crowdfunding Dips its Toe in AIM." *AIM Journal* April 2016: 10. Web. 16 November 2016.

"Crowdfunding Meets the Mining Sector." *International Mining*. International Mining, 4 November 2015. Web. 16 November 2016.

"The Current State of Crowdfunding in the UK." *CrowdfundingHub*. CrowdfundingHub, n.d. Web. 16 November 2016.

"FCA Handbook." FCA. Financial Conduct Authority, n.d. Web. 2 August 2016.

"Finance & Taxation Policy: Super Flow-Through Program." *PDAC*. Prospectors & Developers Association of Canada, n.d. Web. 10 September 2016.

"Flow-Through Shares (FTSs)." *Canada Revenue Agency*. Canada Revenue Agency, n.d. Web. 8 September 2016.

Garvey, Paul. "Mining Executives Turn to Crowd Funding for Junior Miners." *The Australian*. News Limited, 2 November 2015. Web. 15 November 2016.

Gilbert, Chris. "Mineral Intelligence – Strategic Alignment with Equitise." *LinkedIn*. LinkedIn Corporation, 2 November 2015. Web. 16 November 2016.

"Going Public in Canada." *Miller Thomson*. Miller Thomson LLP, 2011. Web. 21 September 2016.

"A Guide to AIM." *London Stock Exchange*. London Stock Exchange Group plc., 2010. Web. 31 July 2016.

"A Guide to AIM." *London Stock Exchange*. London Stock Exchange Group plc., 2015. Web. 31 July 2016.

"Guide to Listing." *TMX*. TSX Inc., 2016. Web. 11 September 2016.

"How PrimaryBid Aims to Give Investors a Better Deal." *Growth Company Investor*. Growth Company Investor Ltd, 31 March 2016. Web. 16 November 2016.

"How the Flow-Through Share (FTS) Program Works." *Canada Revenue Agency*. Government of Canada, n.d. Web. 10 September 2016.

"Instructions for the Flow-Through Share Program." *Canada Revenue Agency*. Government of Canada, n.d. Web. 10 September 2016.

"Investor Bulletin: Accredited Investors." *U.S. Securities and Exchange Commission*. U.S. Securities and Exchange Commission, 23 September 2013. Web. 16 September 2016.

"Investor Bulletin: Private Placements Under Regulation D." *U.S. Securities and Exchange Commission*. U.S. Securities and Exchange Commission, 23 September 2014. Web. 16 September 2016.

"Investor Publications – Rule 144: Selling Restricted and Control Securities." *U.S. Securities and Exchange Commission*. U.S. Securities and Exchange Commission, 16 January 2013. Web. 16 September 2016.

Koven, Peter. "How Crowdfunding Site Klondike Strike Is Changing the Way Junior Miners Raise Money." *Financial Post*. National Post, 18 April 2016. Web. 17 November 2016.

"Listing Requirements." *ASX*. ASX Limited, n.d. Web. 11 September 2016.

"Markets: UK Listing Authority (UKLA)." *FCA*. FCA, n.d. Web. 2 August 2016.

"Metals & Mining Sector Profile." *ASX*. ASX Limited, 2015. Web. 31 July 2016.

"The MiG Report, June 2016." *MiG Market Intelligence Group*. TSX Inc., June 2016. Web. 31 July 2016.

"Mineral Exploration Tax Credit." *Natural Resources Canada*. Government of Canada, 27 April 2016. Web. 8 September 2016.

Mineral Intelligence. *Crowdfunding Meets the Mining Sector as Mineral Intelligence Launches Global Mining Portal*. West Perth: Mineral Intelligence, 2 November 2015. Web. 16 November 2016.

"Mining-Specific Tax Provisions." *Natural Resources Canada*. Government of Canada, 11 April 2016. Web. 10 September 2016.

"Multilateral CSA Notice of Publication and Request for Comment Proposed Multilateral Instrument 45-109 Prospectus Exemption for Start-Up Businesses." *CSA*. Canadian Securities Administrators, 19 October 2015. Web. 16 November 2016.

"Multilateral Instrument 45-108 Crowdfunding." *Ontario Securities Commission*. Ontario Securities Commission, n.d. Web. 16 November 2016.

"The Official List (Listed Companies)." *ASX*. ASX Limited, n.d. Web. 31 July 2016.

"PrimaryBid Announces a £500,000 Fund Raising for Ascent Resources plc." *London Stock Exchange*. London Stock Exchange plc, 1 June 2016. Web. 16 November 2016.

"A Review of the Regulatory Regime for Crowdfunding and the Promotion of Non-Readily Realisable Securities by Other Media." *FCA*. Financial Conduct Authority, February 2015. Web. 16 November 2016.

Robertson, Stephen P. and Pascal de Guise. "Canadian Securities Regulators Publish Crowdfunding Exemption." *NCFA*. National Crowdfunding Association of Canada, 2 December 2015. Web. 16 November 2016.

"Sector and Product Profiles: Global Leaders in Mining." *TMX*. TSX Inc., n.d. Web. 30 July 2016.

"Small Business and the SEC." *U.S. Securities and Exchange Commission*. U.S. Securities and Exchange Commission, 1 February 2016. Web. 16 September 2016.

"Super Flow-Through Shares, Mineral Exploration Tax Credit (METC) Brochure." *PDAC*. Prospectors & Developers Association of Canada, January 2016. Web. 10 September 2016.

Tarikh, Salma. "Red Cloud Revitalizes Mining Investment." *The Northern Miner*. The Northern Miner Group, 28 March 2016. Web. 18 July 2016.

"Toronto: The World's Strategic Hub for Mining Finance." *TMX*. TSX Inc., 22 September 2015. Web. 21 September 2016.

"TSXV Corporate Finance Policies: Policy 2.4—Capital Pool Companies." *TSXV Corporate Finance Manual.* TSX Inc., 14 June 2010. Web. 3 August 2016.

United States. Congressional House of Representatives. *Jumpstart Out Business Startups* Act. 112th Congress, 2nd Session. HR 3606. Washington: GPO, 2012. Web. 20 August 2016.

Wilson, James. "Silver Wheaton Pioneers Payment Streams for Miners." *Financial Times.* The Financial Times LTD., 19 January 2014. Web. 31 July 2016.

Made in the USA
Monee, IL
07 October 2020